HOW TO MAKE AND PLAY
PAN-PIPES

Alvaro Graña

**Published by Condor Books
Lima & Coventry**

3 Broadway - Earlsdon - Coventry - West Midlands
CV5 6NW

*To my children
Natalia and Orlando Graña
and all Andean People*

PAN-PIPES
THE MAGIC SOUND OF THE ANDES

5   1   A GENERAL BACKGROUND TO ANDEAN MUSIC

6   2   ABOUT THE INSTRUMENTS

6   3   FOR THE MUSICALLY MINDED

7   4   THE HUAYNO

9   5   THE ANDEAN PAN-PIPES
           The various sizes and names.
           The notes.

13   6   HOW TO MAKE A SET OF ANDEAN PAN-PIPES / step by step

19   7   HOW TO PLAY THE ANDEAN PAN-PIPES
           The breathing
           How to produce the sound
               The right position of the instrument
               The direction of the flow of air
               The attack to the sound.

22   8   MUSIC SCORES
           Playing music with the Andean pan-pipes
              The "Number Method".
              Tunes and songs in music scores.

9   BIBLIOGRAPHY, RESOURCES & MOCHICA REFERENCE

The drawings shown below and on the front cover have been extracted from a vase of the Mochica Culture (*100 B.C. - 700 A.D.*). The vase, currently held by the Ethnological Museum of Berlin, depicts a group of musicians who belong to a high social group. Note that the two pan-pipe players are taller and have better clothes than the other two.

You can see that the pan-pipes have hand-shaped appendages, according to E. Benson these suggest that the instrument was used in ceremonies related to "the cut of hands" where the hands of persistent thieves were amputated!

The musician on the left has a pan-pipe "IRA" and a hat which is shaped like a Jaguar. The other player, with the pan-pipe "ARCA" has a bird-shaped hat. E. Benson states that these hats are a representation of a god and his artful helper (or priest). Both are depicted in other drawings and are always together. It is possible that the artful helper is the divinity's double. This duality was applied to the set of pan-pipes.

from "The Musical Dialogue: The Technique of the Sikus" - Américo Valencia Chacón

MOCHICA ICONOGRAPHY / Musicians / 100 BC-700 AD / Perú

1 A GENERAL BACKGROUND TO ANDEAN MUSIC

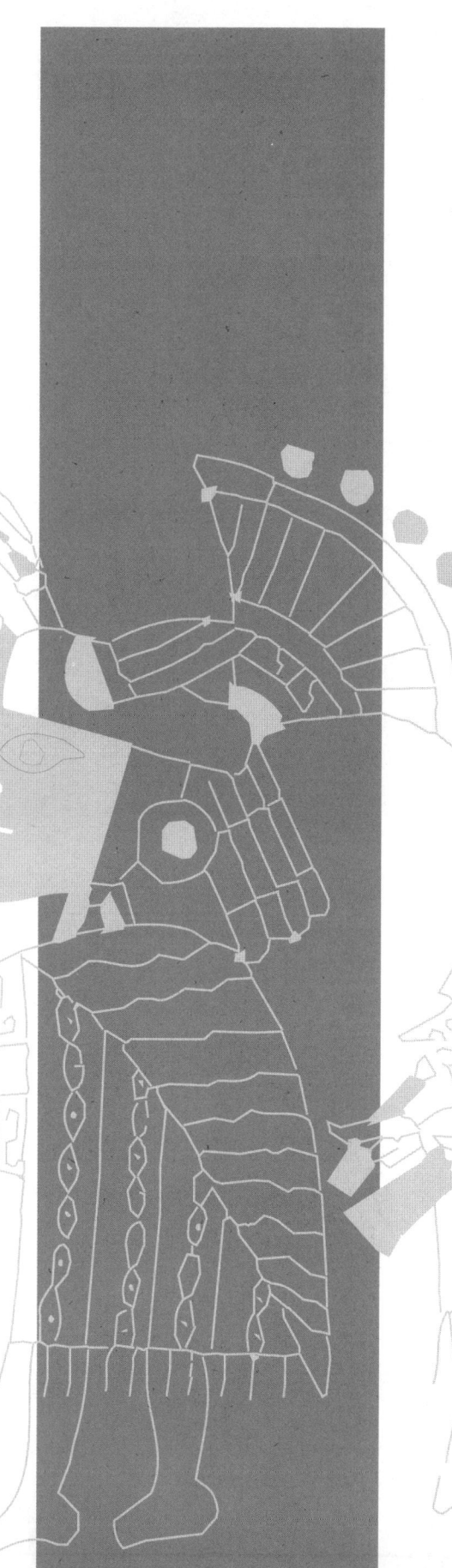

Music exists in every culture as a very important way of expressing feelings and thoughts about daily life. Even though music is something you can do on your own, it also has a social purpose. It can often be shared and enjoyed with others.

In the past musicians had an important role. This was not only to entertain people while they worked but musicians would also be asked to attend other gatherings: to ease their communication with gods or to bring them closer together when sharing happiness or sadness. This would be on occasions such as religious ceremonies, weddings, childbirth, death and harvest-time. Sometimes they would be asked to use their talents to bring comfort during times of illness.

The music of ancient people from the Andes has been brought down from generation to generation, traditionally by word of mouth. We can imagine how that early music sounded since the music that the Quechuas and the Aymaras play today is probably very similar to it. Amazingly, some of the instruments being used today are almost unchanged since pre-Inca times. We know this because instruments have been found in tombs and similar burial places. Experts have analysed and dated them. These are of two kinds: wind and percussion. Stringed instruments were unknown. It was the Spaniards who introduced these instruments, namely guitar, violin, harp and mandolin, all of which are used today to play traditional music.

Among the percussion instruments were: drums, rattles and bells. Wind instruments included flutes, whistles and horns. Flutes with finger holes (known in the Andes as Quenas) produced several tones but the pan-pipes, being more unusual, are of special interest and importance.

2 ABOUT THE INSTRUMENTS

Pre-Columbian cultures of South America seem to have had an active life judging by the impressive and interesting selection of musical instruments excavated from prehistoric ruins. Pan-pipes, flutes, whistles, rattles, drums and trumpets made out of either mud, pottery, shell, bone, wood or metal (including gold) were found. For instance in the Province of Lima, Perú, a set of pan-pipes and a quena (flute) were found and dated 7,000 years old. Whistles made out of mud and bone found in Kotosh (Huanuco, Perú) have been dated 4,500 years old.

All these instruments correspond to a period in which clay was still unknown. Only stone, mud and organic material were used as raw materials for making tools and other objects. It is assumed they also used bamboo canes. Indeed this is the material most used nowadays.

The people made their instruments with materials which were readily at hand. Flutes were made from bones and mud; pan-pipes from reeds; the charango from the shells of armadillos; drums were hollowed out of tree trunks and covered with goatskins. Shakers were made out of goat's hooves.

3 FOR THE MUSICALLY MINDED

There is a great range of local traditions in the large and extended region of the Andes. Each region has developed and encouraged its own individual style of music playing as well as singing and dancing. We can see the same in other large regions of the world.

A lot of the pre-Columbian music has the pentatonic structure, which is the 5 note scale represented by the 5 black keys of the piano keyboard. If the tonic is placed on F sharp ($F^\sharp$), the scale is major; and if on D sharp, minor. With the arrival of the Spaniards this scale was extended to 7 notes.

Another important characteristic of Andean music is its syncopated rhythm[*], which may be to do with (or have been influenced by) the breath attack required in playing the pan-pipes.

[*] see figure 1 page 7

4 THE HUAYNO

The most important and representative Andean rhythm is the HUAYNO, which was originally used at funeral processions of the Quechua Indians. Nowadays it is the most popular dance of a vast area of the Andes, which covers Perú, Ecuador, Bolivia and the north of Chile. The huayno has numerous local variations according to the region. These include variations in the choreography, the instruments used and the way it is danced. One bolivian dance of the huayno type for instance is the CACHARPAYA (a very well known tune in this country, which got into the top ten in the charts). Cacharpaya means, in the language of the Quechua and Aymara Indians, "good-bye" or "farewell".

Another variation of this rhythm is the PANDILLA from Puno (Perú), an Andean town that sits by Lake Titicaca. This is the highest navigable lake in the world. The Pandilla starts with a very slow rhythm and finishes in a fast tempo. A combination of two types of instrument is used: the traditional Andean wind instruments - the pan-pipes and the quena (an Indian flute) and representing the stringed instruments, the guitar, mandolin and charango (a ten stringed instrument - the Andean version of the Spanish guitar).

Finally, there is one more huayno variation worthwhile mentioning, the HUAYLAS. The huaylas is from the Huancayo region of Perú in the central Andes. It has very strong syncopation. The instruments used are: the Andean harp, the guitar, the mandolin, the saxophone and the clarinet. The huaylas is the most powerful and contagious rhythm of them all.

The huayno rhythm is very catchy, whether it is in its fast tempo and very jolly or in its' slow tempo with its strong syncopated rhythm.*

Figure I

HUAYNO rhythm

SYNCOPATED HUAYNO rhythm

* "Syncopation is the displacement of the normal rhythm accent from the strong beat of a bar to one that usually carries a weak beat. This can be achieved by marking weak notes with a stress mark, by replacing normally stressed notes by rests or by holding over a note that first occurs on a weak beat to an accented position."

Dictionary of Music
The Hamlyn Publishing Group Ltd.
Ed.: A. Issacs and E. Martin

Traditional Pan-pipe Players
from the Titicaca Lake Region

Photograph: Fanal Magazine

5 THE ANDEAN PAN-PIPES

The pan-pipes are a type of flute, also known as a 'flute de pan'. How do they work? Well, the sound made by all flutes is basically produced by air striking a hard edge. The simplest way of demonstrating this is by blowing across a pen-top, or a bottle. The pitch of the note varies according to the size of the tube or bottle, the longer ones producing lower sounds.

The pan-pipes, or syrynx, have been found in other ancient cultures around the world. In China where they were called Siao. In Egypt, Syria, South-East Asia, Rumania they are known as the Nai. They have also been found in Rome, Papua New Guinea and New Zealand. In Ancient Greece of course, it was a popular instrument, and according to Greek mythology a set of pipes was thought to have been played by the god Pan - this is where the western world derives the name 'Pan-Pipes'.

In South America, the zampoña (pronounced sampon-ya) is the Spanish name for the instrument, and Siku is the Quechua and Aymara name for it (the two most important local languages in the Andes). Unlike the Nai of Rumania, the zampoña is a set of two rows of pipes, one of 7 pipes called 'ARCA' and the other of 6 called 'IRA'. The pipes are bamboo canes open at one end (into which you blow air) and closed at the other.

Traditionally each set of pipes was played separately by two musicians who had to co-ordinate by alternating notes between them to be able to produce a complete melody, since with just one row of pipes this could not be done. This technique is known as trenzado/trenzando (which means inter-twining) and it is still practised today.

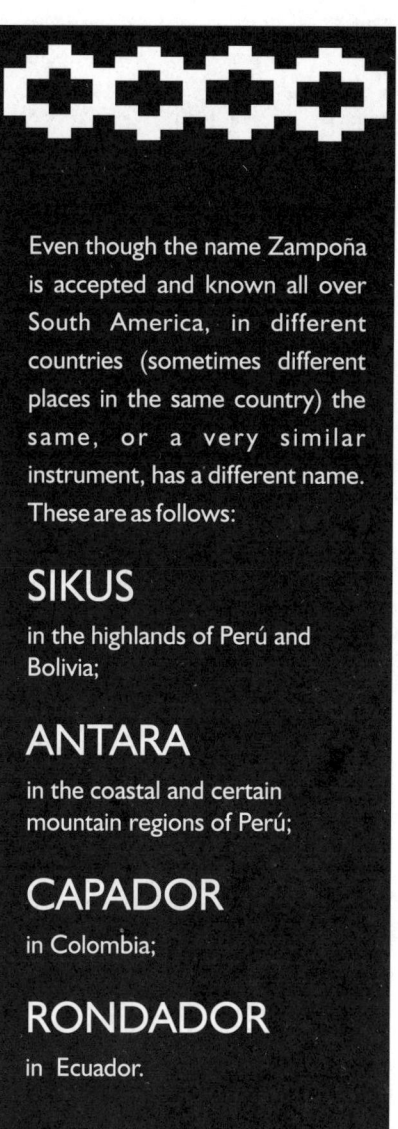

Dancers from "Brisas del Titicaca Cultural Association", Lima, Perú.
Photograph: M. Zubiate

Even though the name Zampoña is accepted and known all over South America, in different countries (sometimes different places in the same country) the same, or a very similar instrument, has a different name. These are as follows:

SIKUS
in the highlands of Perú and Bolivia;

ANTARA
in the coastal and certain mountain regions of Perú;

CAPADOR
in Colombia;

RONDADOR
in Ecuador.

THE VARIOUS SIZES AND NAMES

Zampoña are a set of ARCA and IRA which comes in various sizes, from the smallest called 'Chuli' to the largest set called 'Toyo'. Although zampoña or siku is the generic name for them, each set has its own name. The most popular sets are the 6/7 set and the 12/13 set, the 6/7 being the most common of the two.

We shall be introducing you to just 4 different sizes which are the most representative of this family of instruments. These are:

    The **CHULI**, which is the smallest playable set of zampoñas, and the one with the highest register.

    The **MALTA**, which is the most popular and mostly used as the leading set of pan-pipes in any band.

    The **ZANCA**, which is often used to complement the Malta, either to lead a melody or as a second voice to the Malta.

    The **TOYO**, which is used as the bass, but is capable of playing very haunting mysterious melodies.

In figure 2 below, you will see the 4 sets of zampoñas mentioned. Observe the overlap of notes. You will see that the last 6 notes of one set are the beginning of the next set. Looking at figure 3 on the facing page you can judge the approximate size of each set.

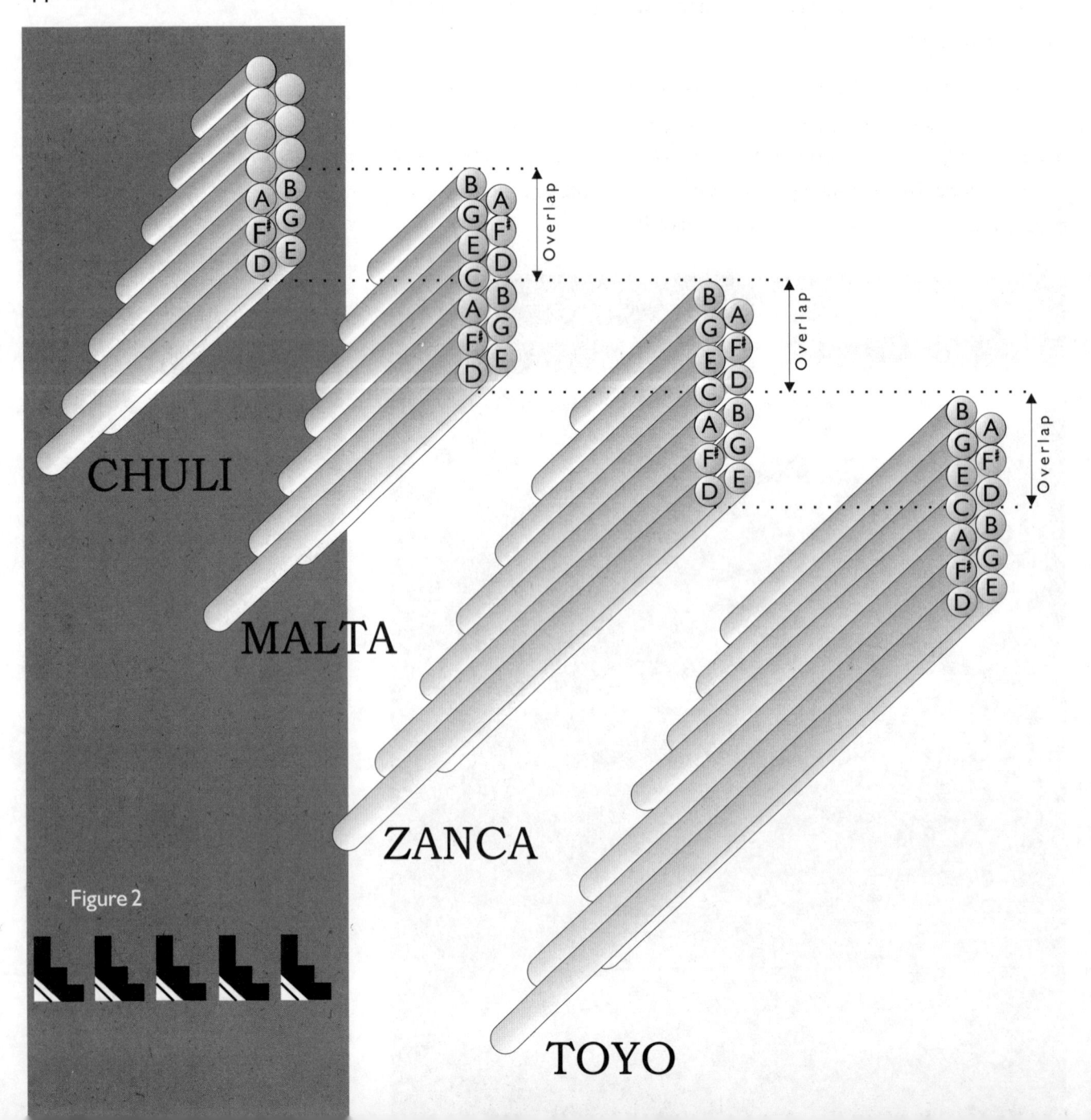

Figure 2

CHULI   MALTA

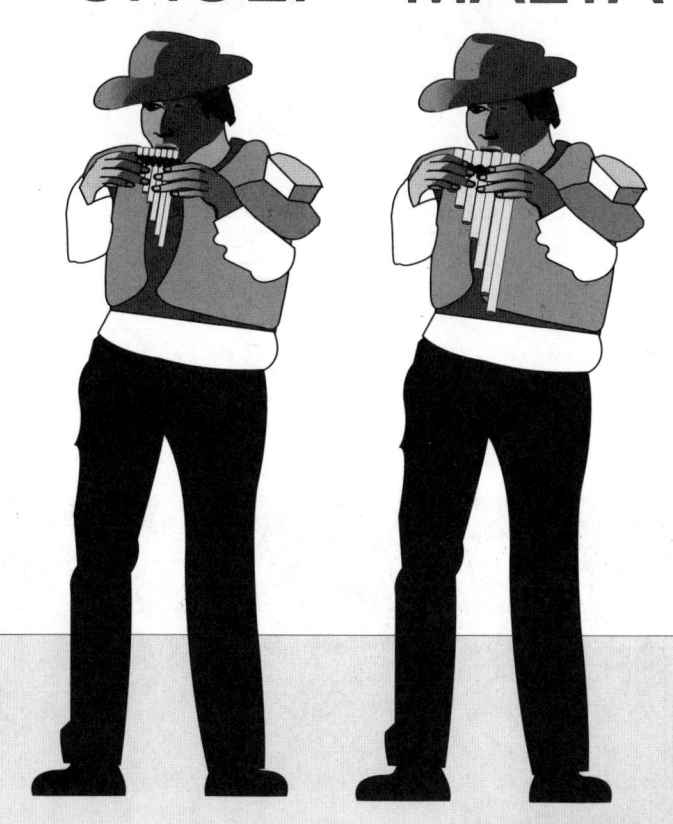

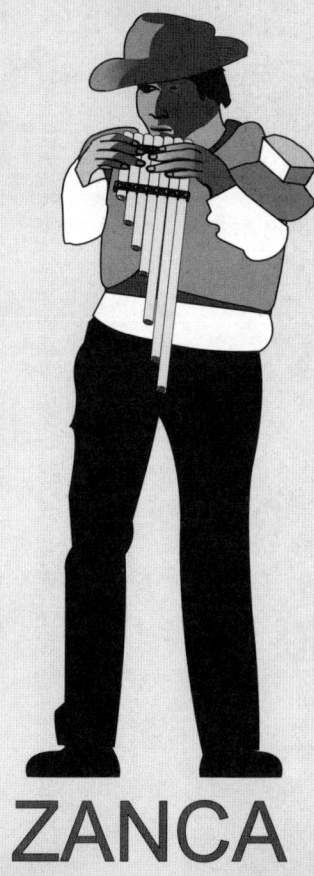

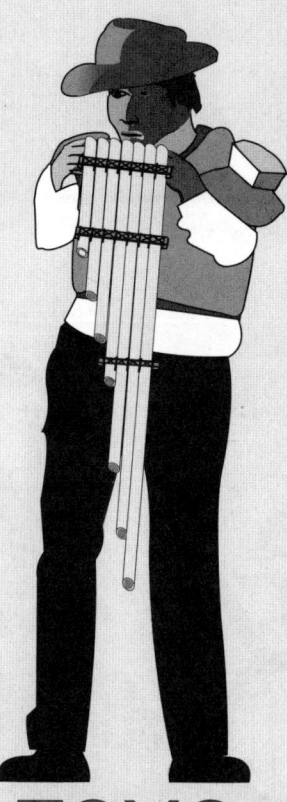

ZANCA   TOYO

Figure 3

THE NOTES

The most common tuning for zampoñas/sikus is in G major, although there are sets tuned in D and in C. The ones you can obtain in this country are mainly tuned in G major.

Figure 4 details the notes on the "zampoña arca" and "zampoña ira" (in G major).

ZAMPOÑA ARCA Ⓓ Ⓕ# Ⓐ Ⓒ Ⓔ Ⓖ Ⓑ

ZAMPOÑA IRA Ⓔ Ⓖ Ⓑ Ⓓ Ⓕ# Ⓐ

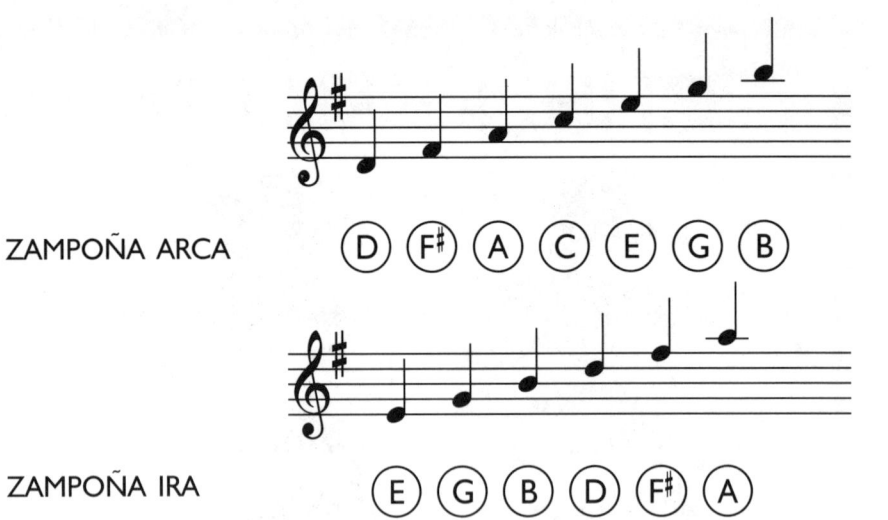

Figure 4

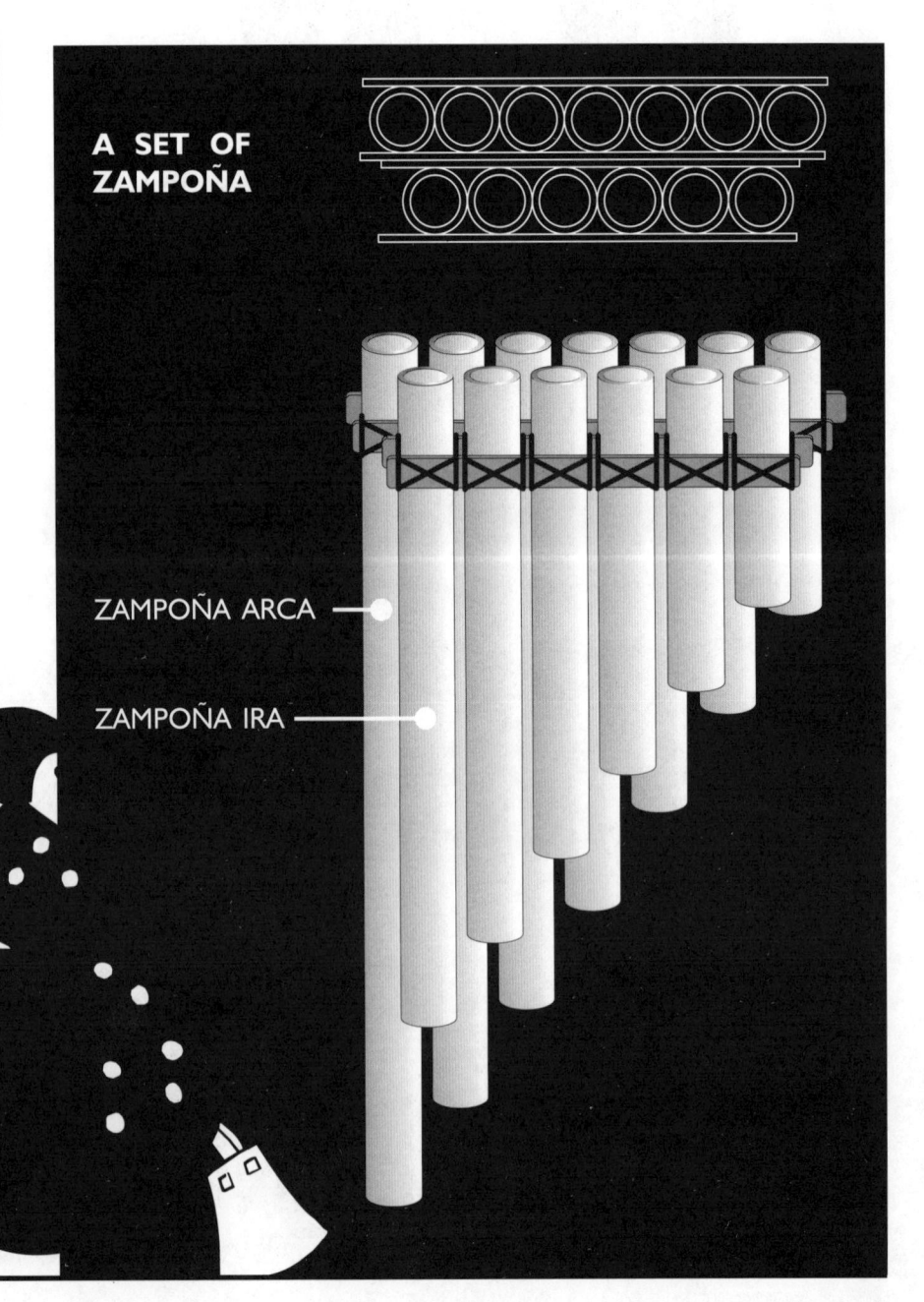

A SET OF ZAMPOÑA

ZAMPOÑA ARCA
ZAMPOÑA IRA

Figure 5

Although practically any sort of tubing will do, I am going to suggest two different ways of making the pan-pipes, using two different types of materials. These two sets will be of very different qualities.

6 HOW TO MAKE A SET OF PAN-PIPES STEP BY STEP

THE FIRST SET

This set is the easiest and cheapest one to make and is ideal for primary school children. It is also safe and fun to make.

You will need the following:

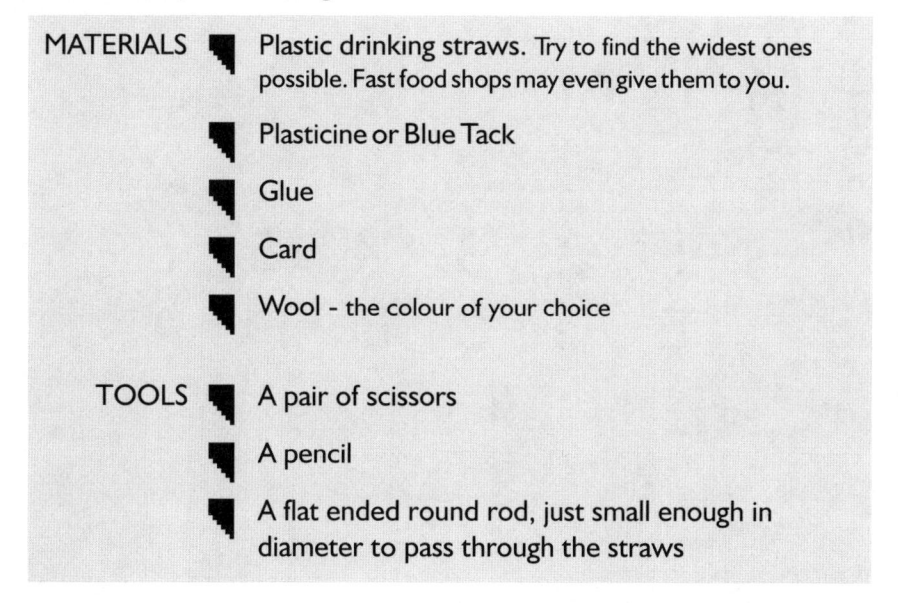

MATERIALS
- Plastic drinking straws. Try to find the widest ones possible. Fast food shops may even give them to you.
- Plasticine or Blue Tack
- Glue
- Card
- Wool - the colour of your choice

TOOLS
- A pair of scissors
- A pencil
- A flat ended round rod, just small enough in diameter to pass through the straws

METHOD   There are three stages in making a set of pan-pipes:

1 Cutting the pipes

2 Tuning the pipes

3 Binding the pipes

1 Cutting the pipes is fairly straight forward. On the next page you will see figure 6 which shows the lengths (actual size) of all the straws you need to cut for 'zampoña arca' and 'zampoña ira'. Simply place the straw on the page, mark the length with a pencil and cut with the scissors. This length is not very critical as fine tuning is done next.

2 To tune the pipes, or straws, you can use either plasticine or blue tack as a stopping medium. I personally prefer blue tack because it is more malleable. Roll a small amount of the material in your hands until it becomes soft. Take a piece small enough to drop into the straw, hold the straw upright on a level surface and insert it into the top. Use the flat ended rod to press it down so that it seals the bottom end of the straw. Take care when you lift the straw from the surface to make sure that the blue tack/plasticine does not stick to the surface.

Blow across the top of the pipe to see what note it produces. You can check the pitch either with a piano or an electronic tuner. This process, adding a little stopping medium and checking the pitch, must be repeated until you obtain the correct note.

Numbers	1	2	3	4	5	6	7
Notes	D	F#	A	C	E	G	B

- 1 D — 15 cm
- 2 F# — 12 cm
- 3 A — 10 cm
- 4 C — 8 cm
- 5 E — 6.3 cm
- 6 G — 5.3 cm
- 7 B — 4.3 cm

Stopping Medium

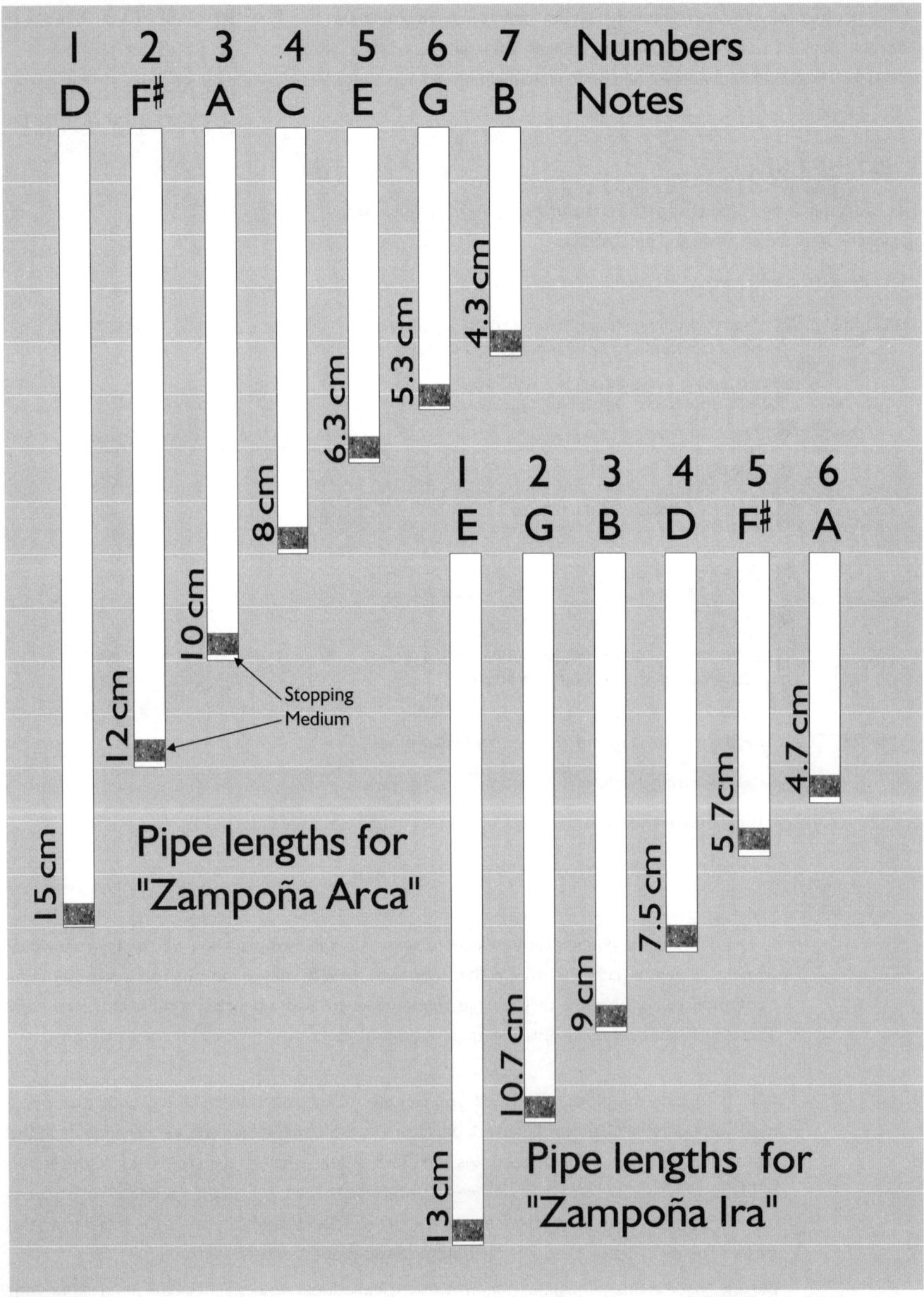

Pipe lengths for "Zampoña Arca"

Numbers	1	2	3	4	5	6
Notes	E	G	B	D	F#	A

- 1 E — 13 cm
- 2 G — 10.7 cm
- 3 B — 9 cm
- 4 D — 7.5 cm
- 5 F# — 5.7 cm
- 6 A — 4.7 cm

Pipe lengths for "Zampoña Ira"

Figure 6

SCALE 1:1 / Actual size

3 Threading the pipes is not as difficult as it looks. You need to thread both the 'zampoña arca' and the 'zampoña ira' separately in a pattern as shown in Figure 7, alternatively you could choose your own pattern. Make sure that the pattern you are doing looks tidy at the front of the zampoña.

Looking at figure 6 you will see that we numbered the pipes of each set. The largest pipe is number one, and on your left as you look at it. You need to cut two identical and narrow pieces of card about one and a half times the total width of the 6 or 7 pipes. Put these at either side of the row of pipes and about 1.5cm. from the top (like a sandwich - see Figure 8 - middle right). Do not worry too much about keeping this distance while you do the binding, at the end you will be able to re-adjust it.

TYING THE FIRST KNOT: We recommend that you bind pipes one and two of the zapmoña ira to begin with. Put the knot on one side, and start from pipe one. Figures 8 and 9 below right show where and how you do the first knot before you start the binding. Leave a good length of thread before the knot because this will be needed for fastening at the end.

There follows is a series of diagrams showing the various stages of the threading process, step by step. The figures show 17 stages, the first 13 take you through the steps to bind two pipes, the next 4 take you to stage 3 for the third pipe and from then on you repeat the same steps until you have all 6 pipes bound together.

You must now repeat this process for the zampoña arca.

Figure 7

Figure 8

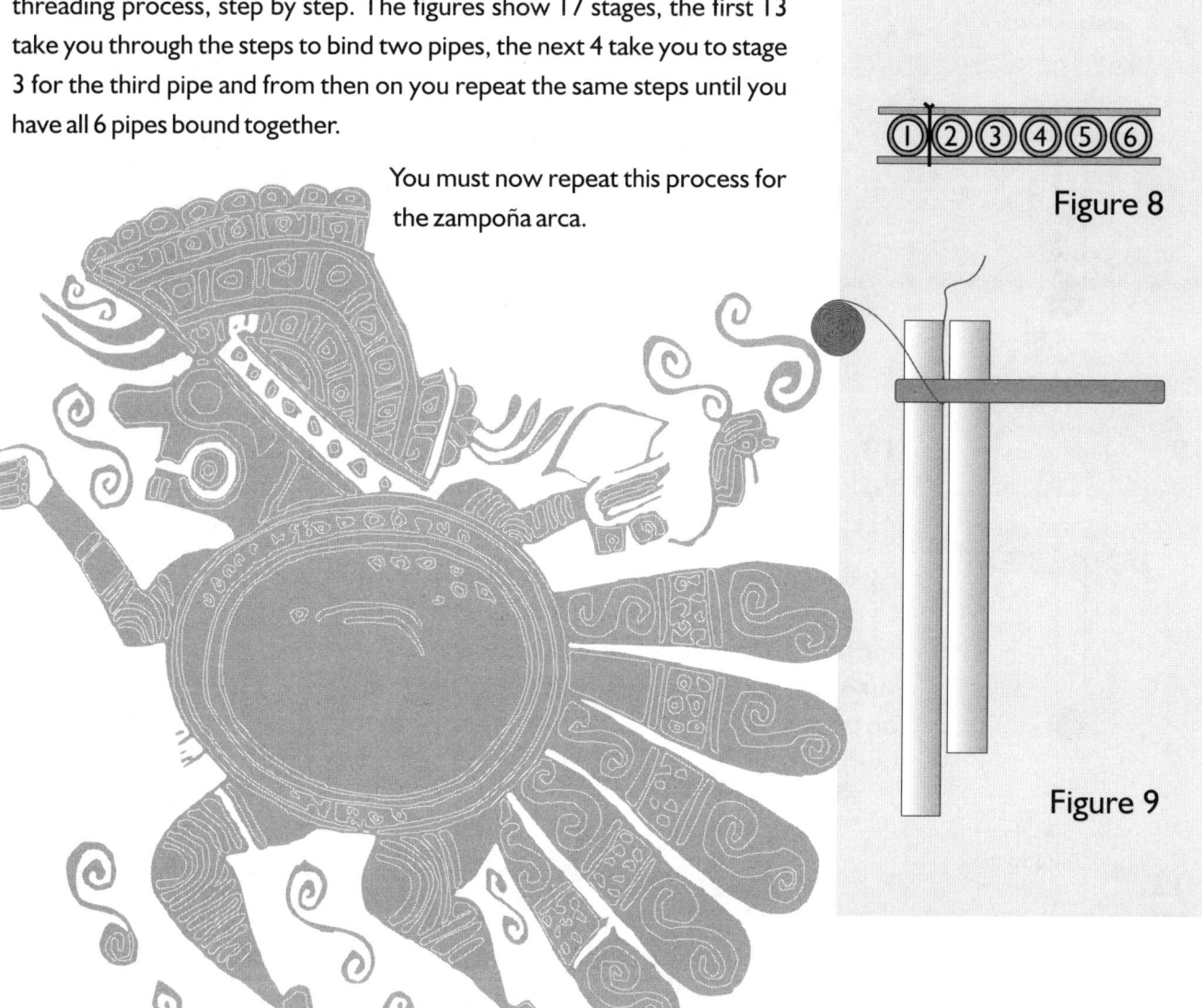

Figure 9

16

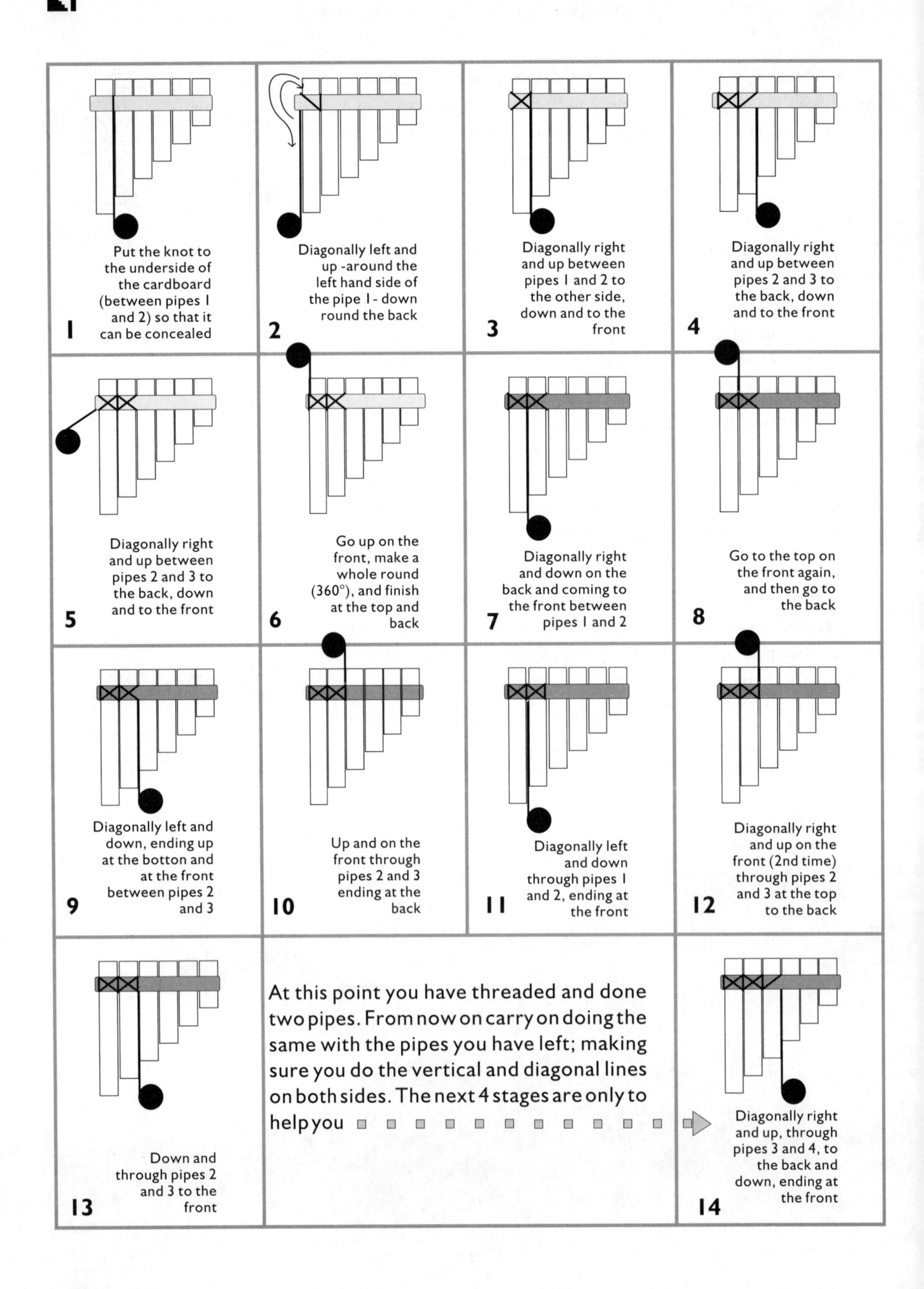

1 Put the knot to the underside of the cardboard (between pipes 1 and 2) so that it can be concealed	**2** Diagonally left and up - around the left hand side of the pipe 1 - down round the back	**3** Diagonally right and up between pipes 1 and 2 to the other side, down and to the front	**4** Diagonally right and up between pipes 2 and 3 to the back, down and to the front
5 Diagonally right and up between pipes 2 and 3 to the back, down and to the front	**6** Go up on the front, make a whole round (360°), and finish at the top and back	**7** Diagonally right and down on the back and coming to the front between pipes 1 and 2	**8** Go to the top on the front again, and then go to the back
9 Diagonally left and down, ending up at the botton and at the front between pipes 2 and 3	**10** Up and on the front through pipes 2 and 3 ending at the back	**11** Diagonally left and down through pipes 1 and 2, ending at the front	**12** Diagonally right and up on the front (2nd time) through pipes 2 and 3 at the top to the back
13 Down and through pipes 2 and 3 to the front	At this point you have threaded and done two pipes. From now on carry on doing the same with the pipes you have left; making sure you do the vertical and diagonal lines on both sides. The next 4 stages are only to help you		**14** Diagonally right and up, through pipes 3 and 4, to the back and down, ending at the front

15 Diagonally left and up through pipes 2 and 3, diagonally right & down the back through pipes 3 and 4 to the front	**16** Up and through pipes 3 and 4 diagonally left and down between pipes 2 and 3 to the front	**17** Diagonally right and up, through pipes 3 and 4 down the back, through pipes 3 and 4 and to the front

FINISHING THE BINDING

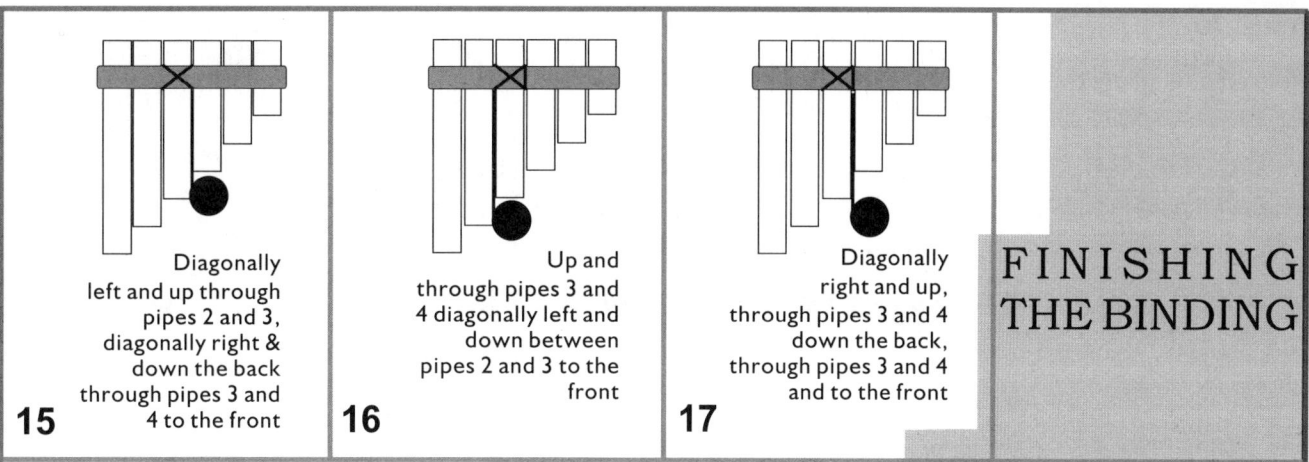

When you have finished binding all the pipes you will need to do a final knot. After binding and tightening up the last pipe, you will have something similar to that shown in Figure 10 - right. There will be the excess thread from your first knot on the left, and the end of your thread on the right. Now, bring the two together and make your final knot (see Figure 11 - below/right).

Finally cut off any excess card and thread you may have. Now readjust the pipes and make sure that the card is at the right distance from the top (1.5cm) as mentioned near the beginning of step 3 (page 15).

Now it is time to have a go at playing them.   GOOD LUCK!

Figure 10

Figure 11

THE SECOND SET

This second set of pan-pipes is of much better quality than the first one. For this set the pipes are made from 15mm plastic piping as used in plumbing.

You will need the following:

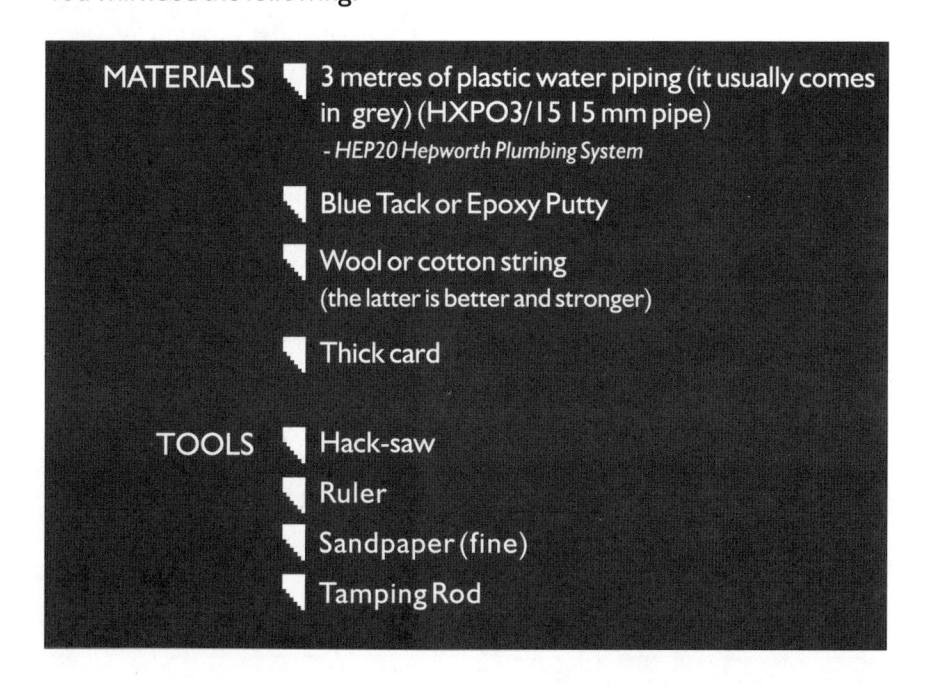

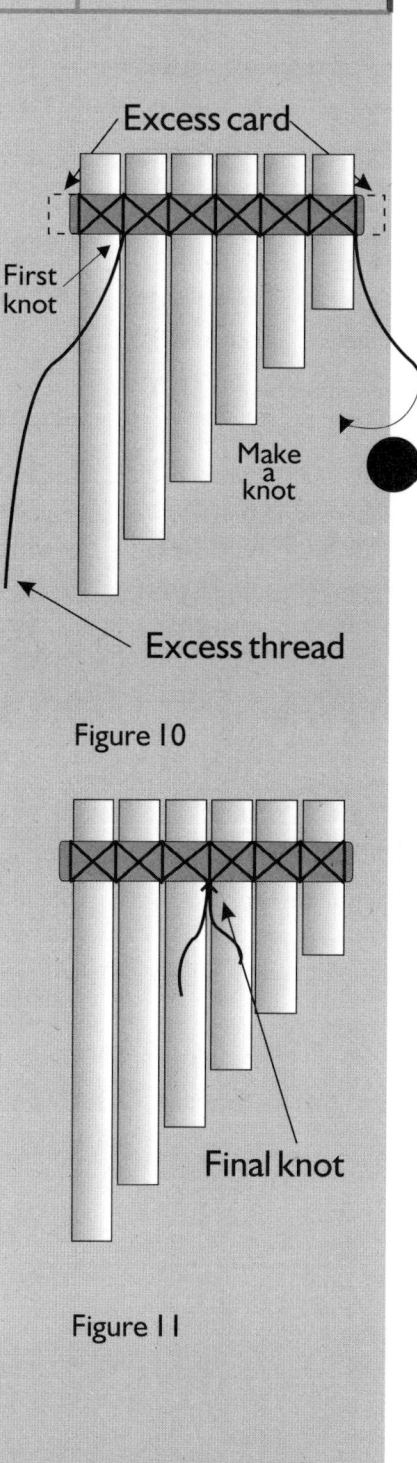

MATERIALS
- 3 metres of plastic water piping (it usually comes in grey) (HXPO3/15 15 mm pipe)
  - *HEP20 Hepworth Plumbing System*
- Blue Tack or Epoxy Putty
- Wool or cotton string
  (the latter is better and stronger)
- Thick card

TOOLS
- Hack-saw
- Ruler
- Sandpaper (fine)
- Tamping Rod

Method

You need to follow the same 3 stages as for the previous set.

1 Cutting the pipes. - To cut the pipes for this set is also fairly easy, but it is not advisable to allow children of primary school age to use the hacksaw by themselves. When cutting the pipes, try to do it as neatly as possible. My recommendation is to do it slowly to avoid leaving the edge too rough. Clean up the sawn ends by rubbing gently with fine sandpaper until smooth.

The pipes need to be cut to the following measurements:

for Zampoña ARCA

Pipe No. 1	(tuned in D)	30cm
Pipe No. 2	(tuned in F#)	24cm
Pipe No. 3	(tuned in A)	21cm
Pipe No. 4	(tuned in C)	18cm
Pipe No. 5	(tuned in E)	14cm
Pipe No. 6	(tuned in G)	12cm
Pipe No. 7	(tuned in B)	9cm

for Zampoña IRA

Pipe No. 1	(tuned in E)	26cm
Pipe No. 2	(tuned in G)	23cm
Pipe No. 3	(tuned in B)	18cm
Pipe No. 4	(tuned in D)	15cm
Pipe No. 5	(tuned in F#)	12cm
Pipe No. 6	(tuned in A)	10cm

2 Tuning the pan-pipes. - Exactly as was done for the first set, the tuning is achieved by stopping up the bottom end of each pipe with a soft material such as Blue Tack or an epoxy (two part) putty such as Milliput. Again a repeat process must be used - adding the stopper, testing the note -until the correct pitch is achieved (see chart above). Remember the more stuffing you put in the higher the note you get.

3 Threading (binding) the pipes.- Again, the process is exactly the same as for the previous set of pan-pipes. Please see diagrams on pages 16 & 17.

Now it is time to play them - GOOD LUCK !

Motif : MOCHICA
Magical Rite. 100BC-700AD
PERÚ

There are two ways of playing the pan-pipes: the first way is 'trenzando' which is the traditional way, as mentioned previously, and the second way is as a set, in other words, playing both zampoña arca and zampoña ira at the same time. The zampoña arca has to be placed furthest away from you and the zampoña ira closest to you. In addition, you have to lower the zampoña ira a little (distance varies according to each individual musician) to make both equally accessible (see Figure 12 below).

YOU NEED TO KNOW that there are two ways of positioning the pan-pipes before you start playing them. One is to hold the zampoña arca and the zampoña ira with the longest pipes (or lower notes) to the right as you look at the set of pipes before playing (still keeping the zampoña arca furthest away from you). This is the traditional way which has been passed on from generation to generation since pre-Columbian times. The other way is by playing them the other way around, with the lower notes to the left. This may seem more natural and appropriate to musicians who are familiar with more recent instruments such as the piano and the guitar, but more important is the fact that the convention when writing musical scales is to have the lower notes on the left. (See Figure 4 on page 12).

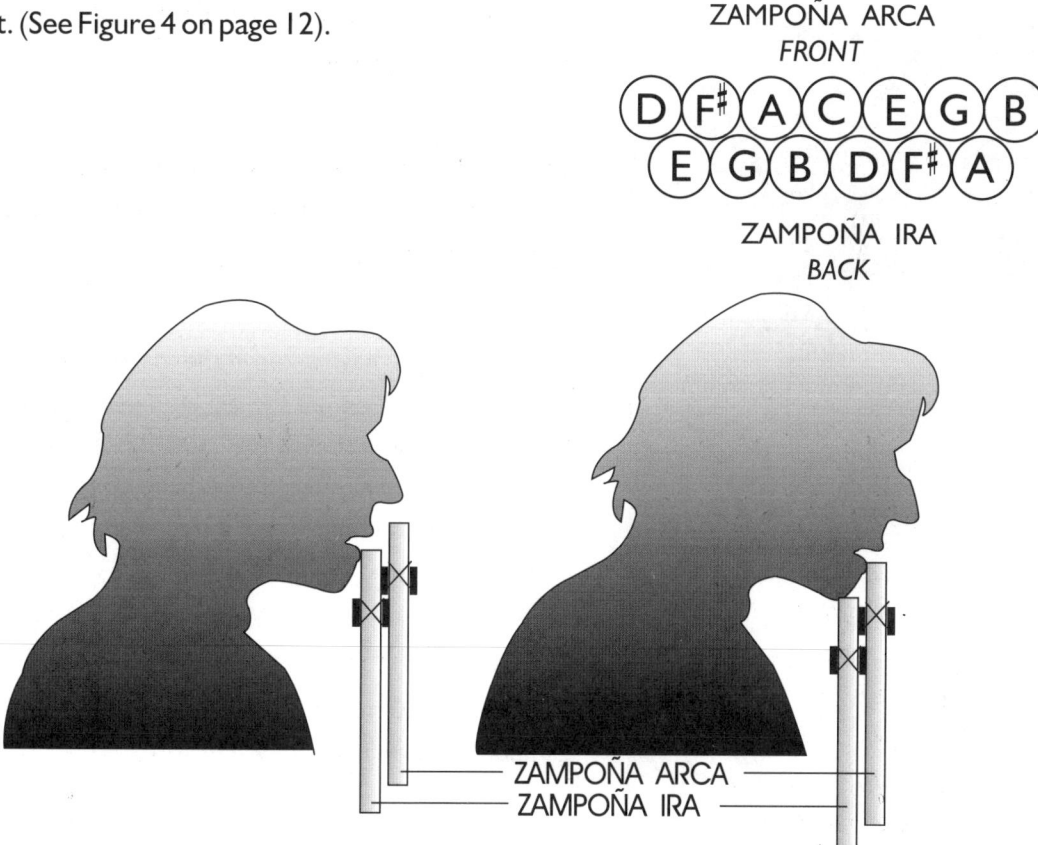

7 HOW TO PLAY THE ANDEAN PAN-PIPES STEP BY STEP

ZAMPOÑA ARCA
FRONT

D F# A C E G B
E G B D F# A

ZAMPOÑA IRA
BACK

Figure 12

This is the zampoña being played as a set seen from the side. The musician has to jump from one row to the other

The Breathing

Before we can start explaining how to play the instrument, we first have to emphasise very strongly the importance of the breathing technique to be used. The breathing controls the amount of air, the strength and quality of the blowing action and the various attacks and arrangements or ways of interpreting the zampoña.

The best breathing technique we recommend is the one used by those who practice yoga, which is sometimes described as the "full breathing technique". A great many musicians use this technique. We shall explain it step by step.

Step 1: Starting from a relaxed standing position, commence inhaling air without expanding your chest (or thorax), as if you have to fill your abdomen with as much air as possible. You should be able to see your abdominal area actually expanding.

Step 2: Continue inhaling air slowly, directing it into the lower ribs and lower back. Here the muscles of your diaphragm come into action, and will be used to control the amount of air you inhale and blow constantly, when you play the zampoña.

Step 3: Finally, as you carry on slowly inhaling more air, you are filling the middle and top part of your lungs. In doing this you will feel and see your chest expanding.

At this point you have taken in the maximum amount of air possible. As an exercise try to keep all the air inside for a few seconds, and then start breathing out very slowly, reversing the 'breathing in' technique explained above. That is to say, first release the air that is on top, pushing from the bottom using your diaphragm muscles, until you release all the air you have stored up. In this process of releasing air you will see your chest becoming smaller first and the lower stomach going in last. You will find that after a few times, your diaphragm may start to ache.

This exercise can also be done using one of the pipes from any of the zampoñas to produce a sustained note.

Be aware that this is an exercise. When you play the zampoña properly and you go from pipe to pipe (or note to note), you have to blow and inhale again and again, always keeping some air in reserve at the bottom of your lungs.

How to produce the sound

To produce the sound in the zampoña you need to blow directly into the open end of the pipe chosen. The quality of the sound will depend on the way you blow. Now that you know the correct breathing technique, you must learn how to obtain the best sound by considering carefully the three factors discussed in the following text.

The right position of the instrument: As shown in figure 12 on page 19, you place the zampoña parallel to your face. You will have to make contact with the pipe to play it. Next, choose the pipe you want to play and place it in the middle of your lower lip. Press it against your lower lip slightly. Now you are ready to blow. The distance between the top of the pipe and your upper lip will depend on the size of the pipe you have chosen to play. A small pipe needs to be closer to your upper lip. As the pipe gets bigger the distance between the pipe and your upper lip increases. In a standard set of pipes this distance is very small. So the principle is the following: the smaller the pipe, the nearer to the upper lip it needs to be.

RECOMMENDATION
You may find it useful to use a mirror to help you see the correct position of the pipes to produce the best sound.

The flow of air: The greater the amount of air going into the pipe the clearer and stronger the sound will be. On the contrary if only a small amount of air is directed into a pipe, and the rest is lost, the quality of the sound will not be very good.

Once you have positioned the instrument correctly as explained above, then you just have to blow, leaving a small gap (or hole) between your lips right in the middle of your mouth. This hole has to be very small to allow the air to come out in the shape of a thin tube (or column) of air. On the other hand you have to remember that the muscles around your mouth must be tense, especially those between your chin and your lower lip. You must particularly remember not to touch the pipe with your upper lip, because you will then block the hole where you are releasing the air and it will no longer produce a sound.

Now it is a matter of trying it again and again; practice makes perfect. I must give you the following warning though: when starting to learn you should do it for short periods of time, otherwise you may become dizzy and if you persist you may even give yourself a headache. With practice this tendency will diminish.

The attack to the sound: This is the final factor to consider, in which the tongue plays an important role. The tongue will act as a stopper. Before you blow a pipe, prior to the attack you should have your tongue positioned so as to close the space between your lips. When you decide to attack (play the note) you pull your tongue back, while at the same time very strongly releasing the amount of air necessary, according to the length of note called for in the music. The use of the muscles in your neck should also be apparent.

This procedure - between the tongue and the blowing action - needs to be well co-ordinated, it is similar to what you do when using the clutch and the accelerator in a car, which involves releasing one and pressing the other.

Playing the pan-pipes following a "method" and/or a standard music score

8 MUSIC IN SCORES

The 'Numbers Method'. The idea of this method is that it is suitable for everybody, regardless of age and musical knowledge. If you read music, you can just follow the scores, having identified where the notes are on the pipes, and then practise, practise practise.

If you do not know how to read music, this method, which we call the 'numbers method', will help you. It is easy to follow:

First of all, we are giving you a few tunes and songs to practice, which you will most likely recognise. By knowing the tune, you will be able to make sense of what you are actually playing.

Secondly, in the first two scores, you will find a little drawing or diagram of a set of pan-pipes just below each note on the score. You will need to blow the pipe which is in black and try to follow the beat of the particular tune or song you are playing.

Thirdly, just below the little drawing, you will find the 'number method'.

This is as follows: Each pipe, as you remember, was given a number from left to right from 1 to 7 for 'zampoña arca' and 1 to 6 for 'zampoña ira'. In this case, to know which pipe to play, instead of following the drawings you follow the numbers.

Remember that as you face the set of pipes to play, the largest pipe(s) should be on your left. Also remember that you could play it holding both sets, or singly with someone else playing the other set (or row of pipes 'arca' or 'ira'). As we mentioned earlier, this is the traditional way of playing the instrument. Here the co-ordination between the two players becomes most important.

For the first and second tunes/songs, you will have the little drawings of the pipes (The Drawing Method), indicating the pipes (notes) to play. After that you will find it unnecessary and following the 'number method' will be a great deal easier. Please see Figure 13 below.

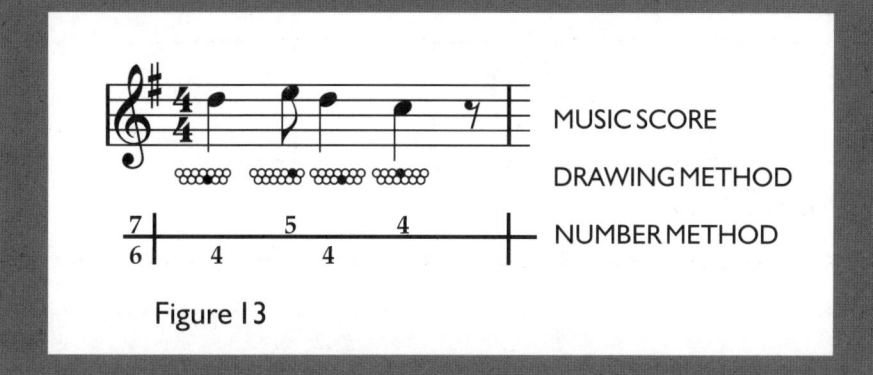

♪ ♪ ♪ 𝄽	MUSIC SCORE
⬡ ⬡ ⬡ ⬡	DRAWING METHOD
7/6 5/4 4	NUMBER METHOD

Figure 13

After practising with tunes and songs that you know, and becoming more familiar with the instrument and more confident, you could try learning a few Andean tunes and songs.

Practice makes perfect! I advise you to practice slowly, taking your time, with the breathing and blowing you have to do. If you are not used to playing a wind instrument, playing for too long will probably make you feel a bit dizzy or give you a headache (because you are using a lot of oxygen). So take your time and give yourself enough rest in between practice periods to recover your oxygen. If you practice enough, you will eventually overcome this problem.

Again, GOOD LUCK!

SOME BASIC MUSIC KNOWLEDGE

We believe that if you are inexperienced, or have never had the chance to learn music, the following concepts might help you to get on when starting to play the music which follows.

Rhythm. - Rhythm is not an easy concept and it cannot be defined in a straightforward way. What we can say is that rhythm is concerned with the 'time' factor in music, especially to do with pulse, stress (or emphasis), and speed - expressions used in music. The pulse is the basic beat of the music and the rhythm is the part which usually fits any words.

Metre.- This is to do with the way music has been structured. Metre is the regular grouping of pulse beats - using accents (stresses) on the first of each group. The most usual groupings are twos, threes and fours. Most Andean music, for example, is in two time, that means with the pulse grouped in twos, like this:

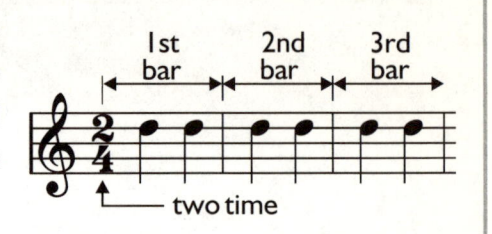

1st bar | 2nd bar | 3rd bar — two time

Stresses.- Within each bar, whether the metre is in 2, 3 or 4 time, the convention is that the first pulse beat of the bar is the strongest and others will be weaker. This is what happens in words, for instance in names you will find stresses, try this one

E -	liz -	a -	beth	Un -	der -	wood	
	*			*			Stresses

←————————— Pulse Beats —————————→

If you repeat this again and again on a regular pulse, you will be saying it in rhythm. Try your own name.

Silence.- Periods of silence are very useful and powerful elements in music. They are called rests, the symbols and their values are as follow:

Semibreve rest — 4 beats

Minim rest — 2 beats

Crotchet rest — 1 beat

Quaver rest — a 1/2 beat

Semiquaver rest — a 1/4 beat

Duration.- This is to do with the lengths of the notes. These are some note names and their values.

Name of note	Symbol	Value
Semibreve	𝅝	a whole note
Minim	𝅗𝅥	a half note
Crotchet	𝅘𝅥	a quarter note
Quaver	𝅘𝅥𝅮	an eighth note
Semiquaver	𝅘𝅥𝅯	a sixteenth note

Here are some more associations of note length and names showing duration:

𝅗𝅥 Tom   𝅘𝅥 𝅘𝅥 Pe-ter   𝅘𝅥𝅮 𝅘𝅥𝅮 𝅘𝅥𝅮 Al-li-son   𝅘𝅥𝅮 𝅘𝅥𝅮 𝅘𝅥𝅮 𝅘𝅥𝅮 Ma-ry John-son

Tie Signs.- A tie is a curved line used in music to link two notes of the same pitch; so you should only sound or play the first note, but it must be held for the length of the two notes being tied.

Repeat Signs.- The repeat sign is a double bar line plus two dots. Music contained between the repeat signs, must be played twice before you move on to the next phrase.

TUNES AND SONGS IN MUSIC SCORES ON THE FOLLOWING PAGES

List of well known songs

1 - London Bridge
2 - Oranges and Lemons
3 - This Old Man
4 - Where Have All the Flowers Gone
5 - My Bonnie Lies Over the Ocean
6 - Yellow Submarine

List of Andean tunes and songs

1 - El Condor Pasa
2 - Floreo de Llamas
3 - Fiesta Aymara
4 - Festival de las Flores
5 - Ojos Azules
6 - Llorando se Fué (also known as 'Lambada')

LONDON BRIDGE

ORANGES and LEMONS

arr. © Condor Books 1995

Traditional English Counting Rhyme

THIS OLD MAN

arr. © Condor Books 1995

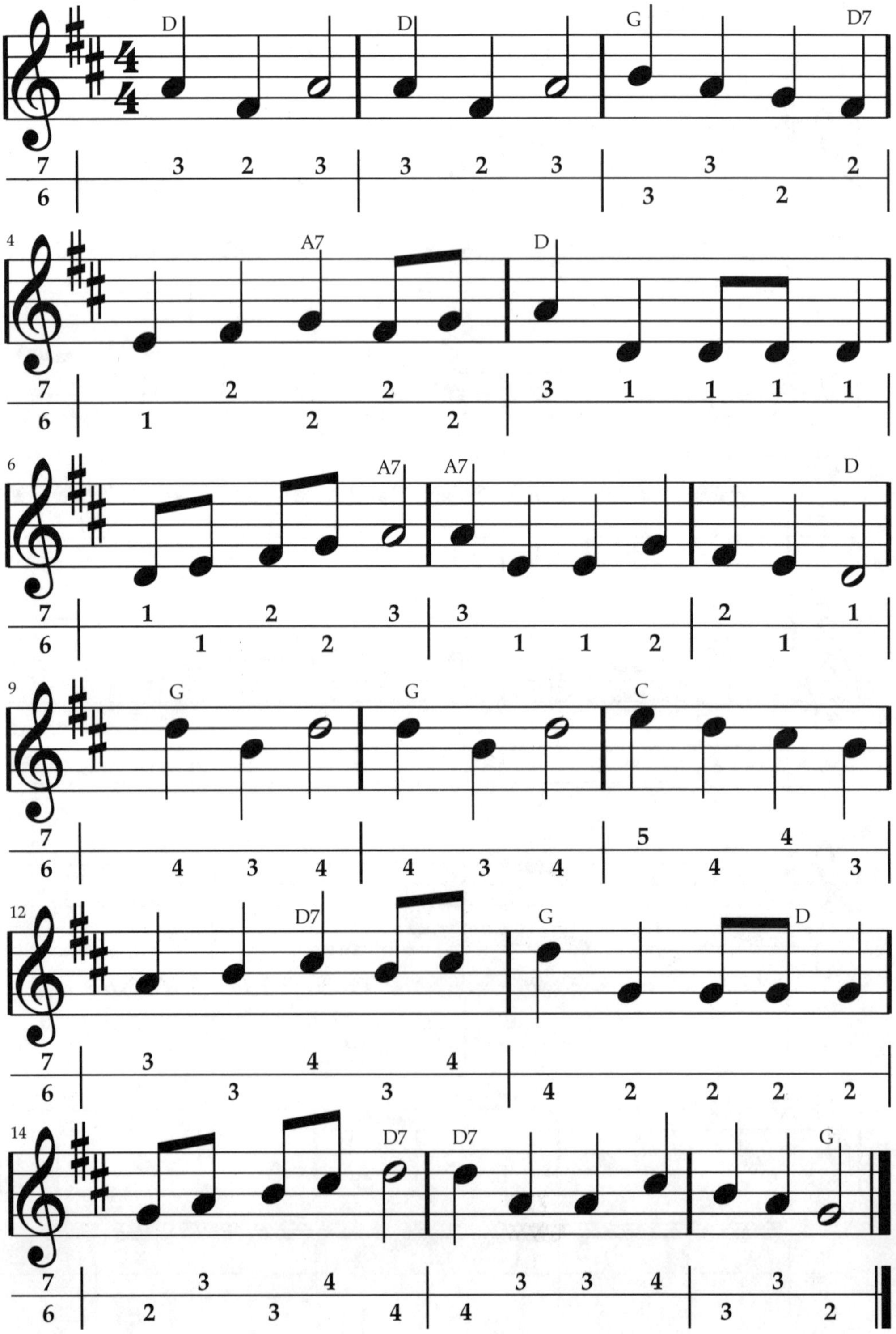

WHERE HAVE ALL THE FLOWERS GONE

Pete Seager   arr. © Condor Books 1995

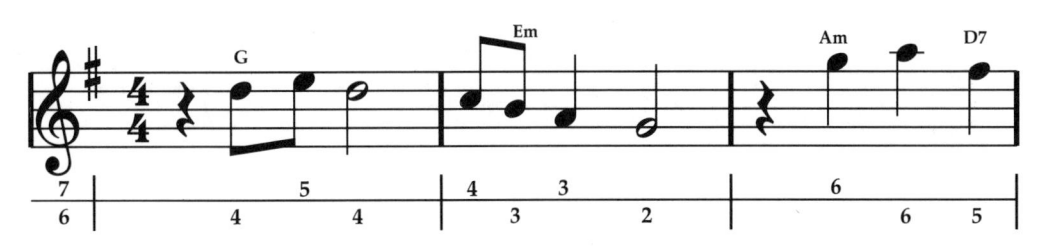

Where have all the flo-wers gone long time pass-

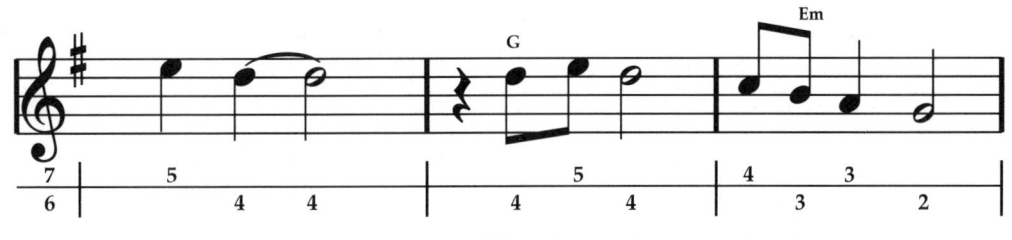

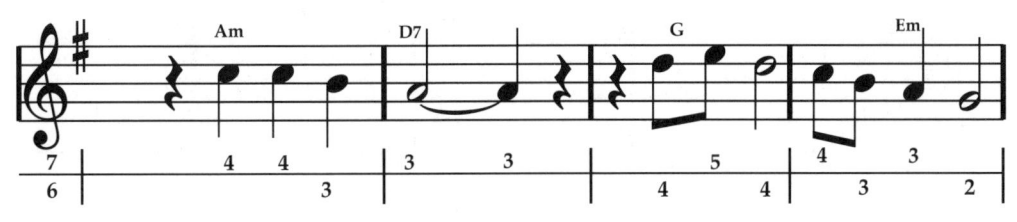

- -ing Where have all the flo-wers gone

long time a - go where have all the flo-wers gone

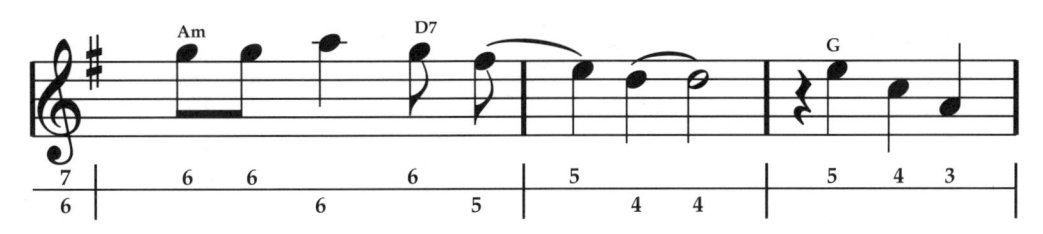

girls have picked them ev - ery one when will they

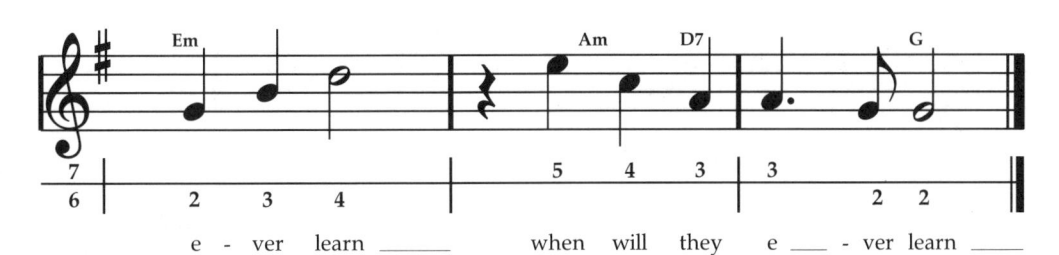

e - ver learn when will they e - ver learn

MY BONNIE LIES OVER THE OCEAN

Traditional North Country arr. © Condor Books 1995

My bon - nie lies o - ver the o - cean ____

My bon - nie lies o - ver the sea ____

My bon - nie lies o - ver the o - cean ____

O bring back my bon - nie to me ____

Bring ____ back ____ bring ____

back _____ O bring back my bon - nie to me _____ to

me _____ bring _____ back _____ bring _____ back O

bring back my bon - nie to me _____

YELLOW SUBMARINE

Lennon-McCartney *arr.© Condor Books 1995*

In the town where I was born lives a ma - a - an *(man)*
So we sailed on to the sun till we fou - ou - ound *(found)*

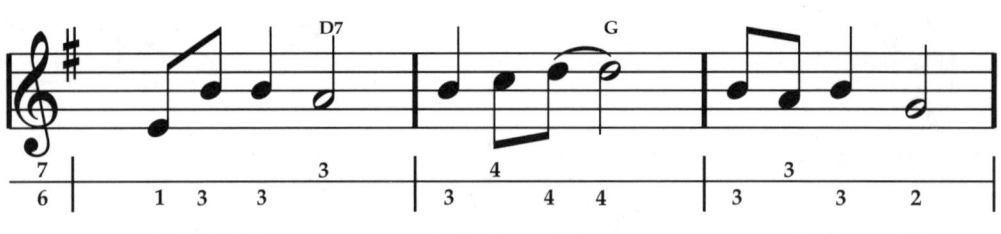

who sailed the sea And he told ___ us of his life
the sea of green And we lived ___ be-neath the sea

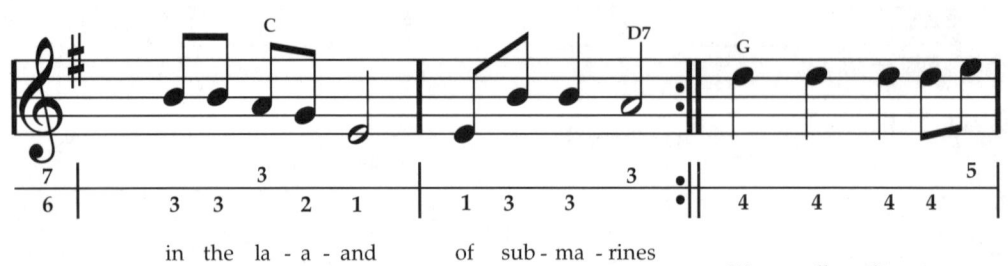

in the la - a - and of sub - ma - rines We all live in a
in our ye - e - ell - - ow sub - ma - rine.

ye-llow sub - ma - rine ye-llow sub - ma - rine ye-llow sub - ma - rine.

EL CONDOR PASA

Daniel Alomías Robles PERU

arr.© Condor Books 1995

FLOREO DE LLAMAS

Traditional South American Folk Song © Condor Books 1995

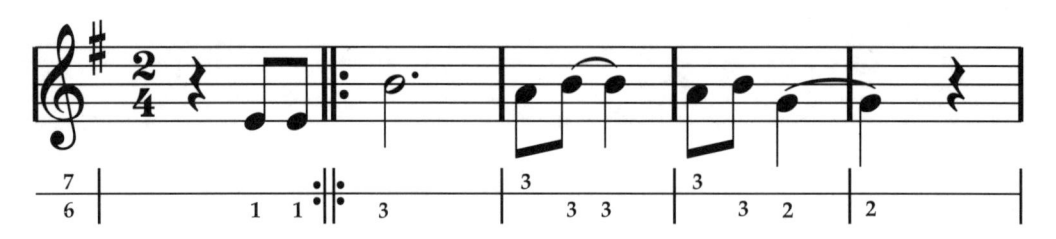

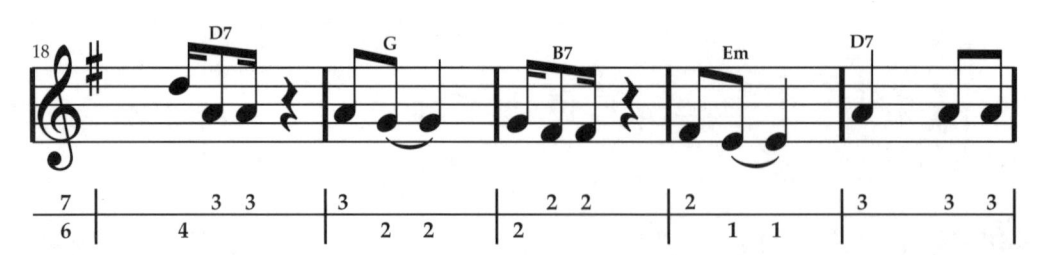

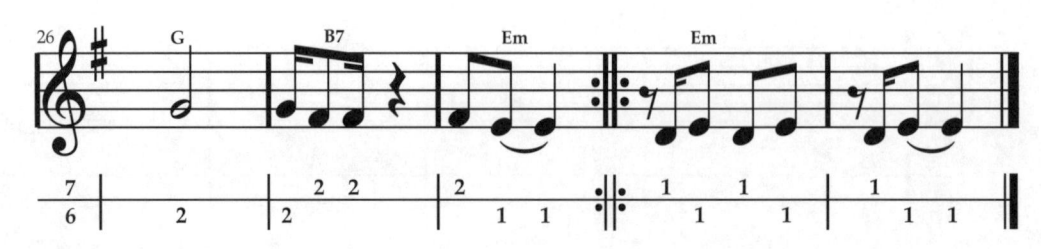

FIESTA AYMARA

Traditional - Huayno - PERU

arr. © Condor Books 1995

FESTIVAL DE LAS FLORES

Alvaro Graña

arr. © Condor Books 1995

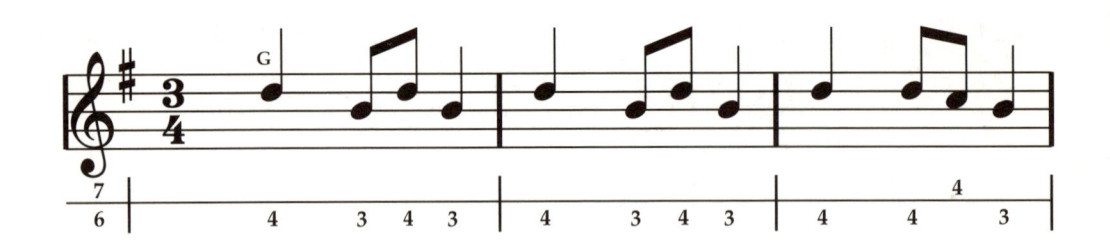

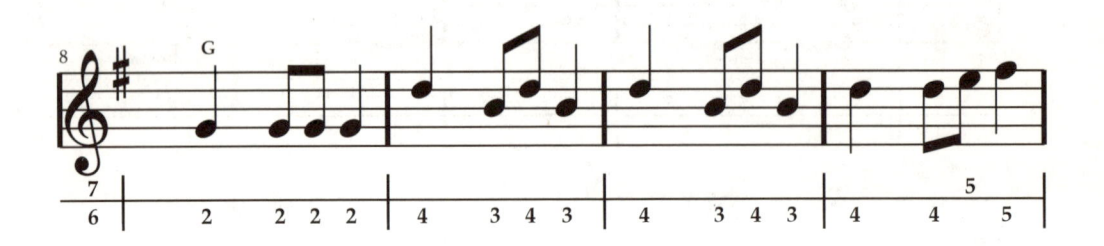

37

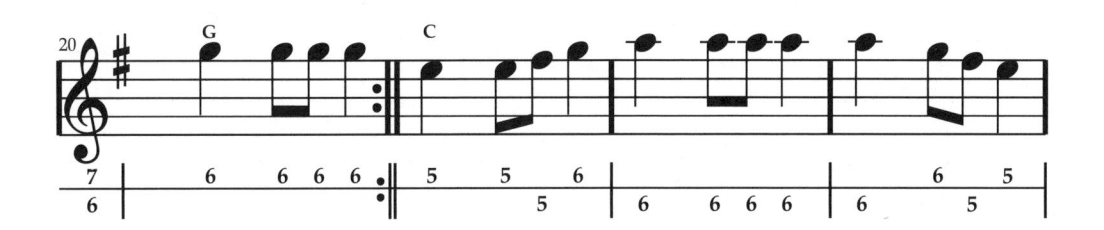

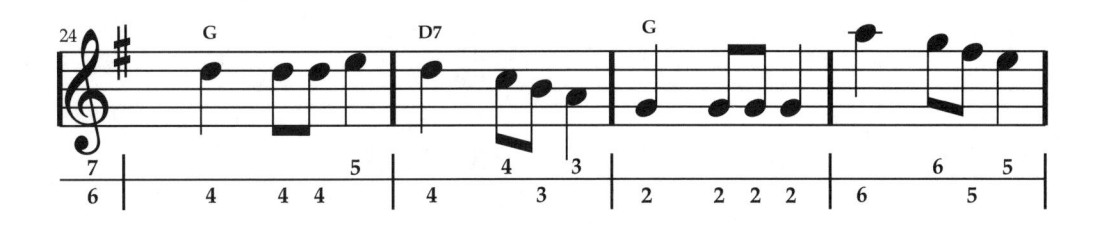

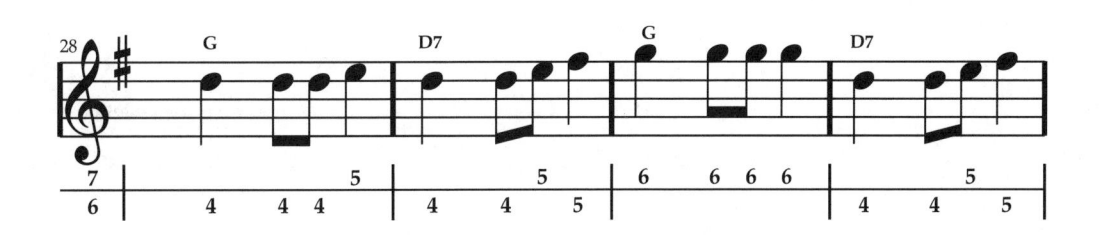

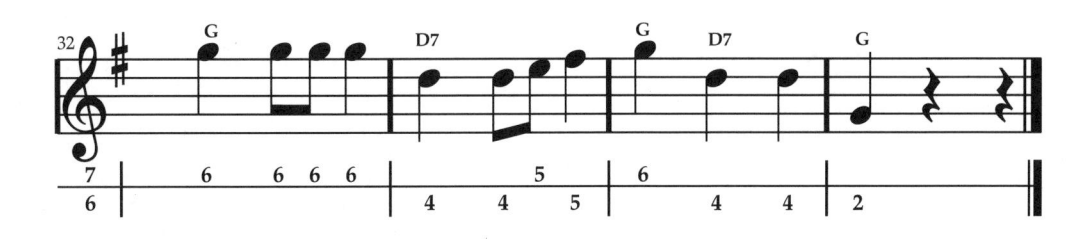

OJOS AZULES

Trote - Traditional - CHILE
arr. © Condor Books 1995

O - jos a - zu - les no llo - res no llo - res ni tee - na - mo - res Llo - ra - ras cuan - do me va - ya cuan - do re - me - dio ya noha - ya.

Tu me ju - ras - te que - rer - me que - rer - me to - da la vi - da No - pa - sa - ron dos tres dí - as tu tea - le - jas y me de jas.

OJOS AZULES - DUET FOR PAN-PIPES

arr. A. Graña

1st voice

2nd voice

1st voice

2nd voice

LLORANDO SE FUÉ

Saya - Ulises Hermosa - BOLIVIA

arr. © Condor Books 1995

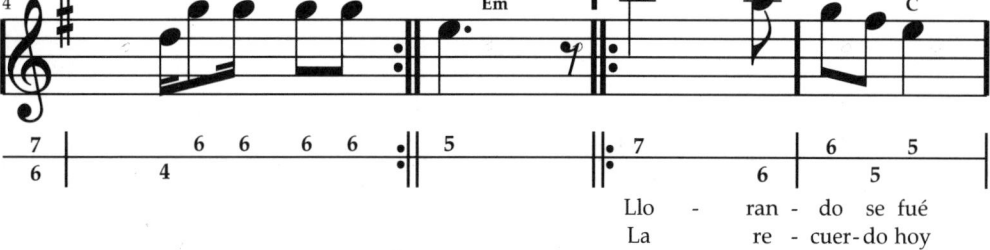

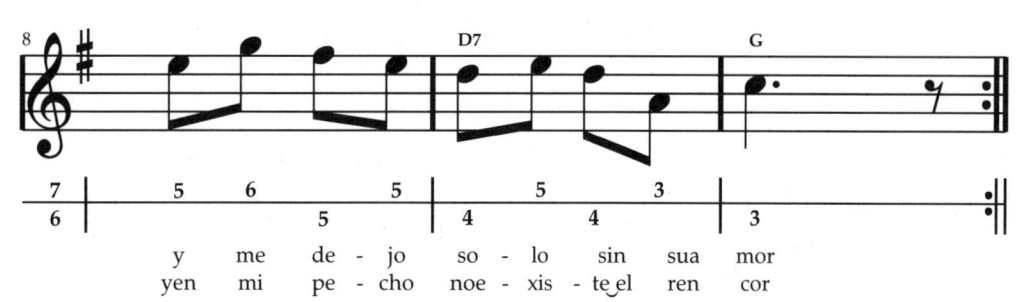

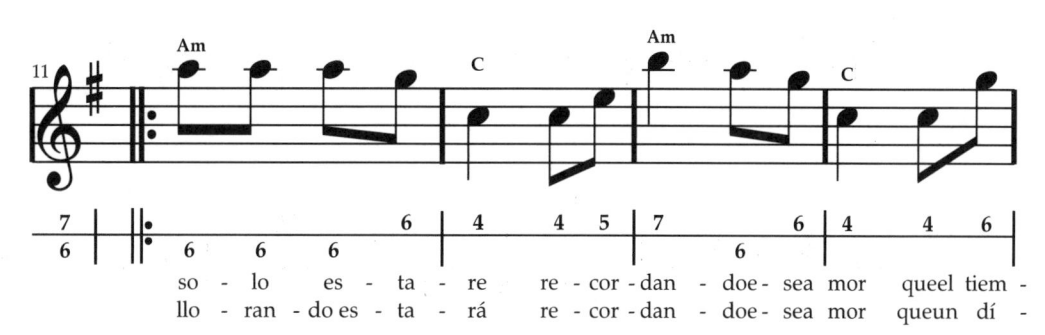

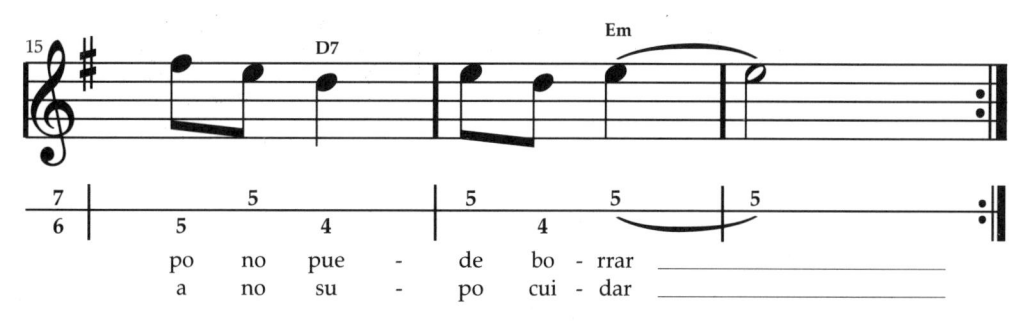

Llo - ran - do se fué
La re - cuer-do hoy

y me de - jo so - lo sin su a mor
yen mi pe - cho no e - xis - te el ren cor

so - lo es - ta - re re - cor - dan - do e - sea mor que el tiem -
llo - ran - do es - ta - rá re - cor - dan - do e - sea mor que un dí -

po no pue - de bo - rrar
a no su - po cui - dar

LLORANDO SE FUÉ - DUET FOR PAN PIPES

Saya - Ulises Hermosa - BOLIVIA
arr. A. Graña

arr. © Condor Books 1995

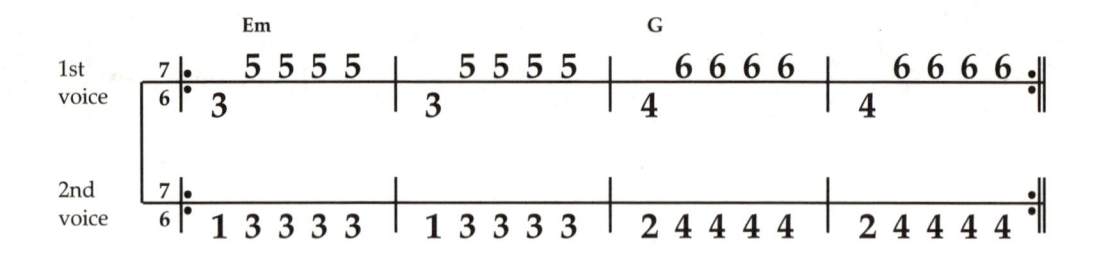

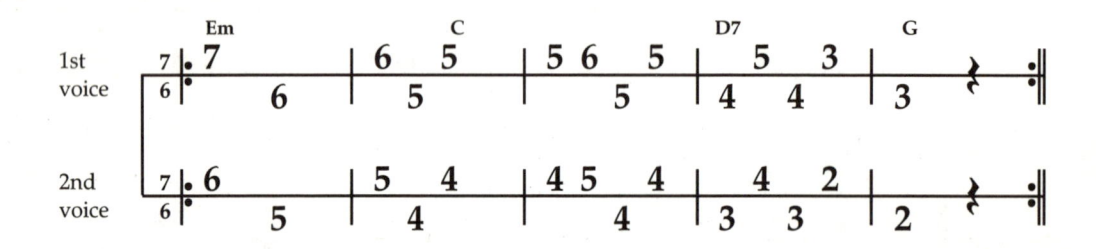

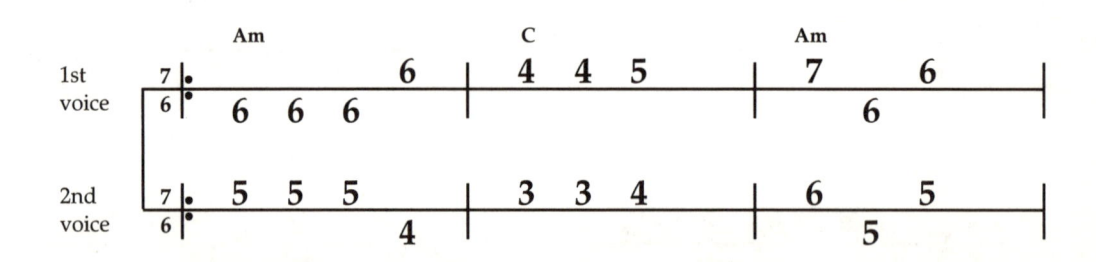

	Em		G	
1st voice	7|. 5 5 5 5	5 5 5 5	6 6 6 6	6 6 6 6 .||
	6| 3	3	4	4
2nd voice	7|. 1 3 3 3 3	1 3 3 3 3	2 4 4 4 4	2 4 4 4 4 .||
	6|			

	Em	C	D7	G
1st voice	7|. 7	6 5	5 6 5	5 3	⸒ .||
	6| 6	5	5	4 4	3
2nd voice	7|. 6	5 4	4 5 4	4 2	⸒ .||
	6| 5	4	4	3 3	2

	Am	C	Am	
1st voice	7|. 6	4 4 5	7 6	
	6| 6 6 6		6	
2nd voice	7|. 5 5 5	3 3 4	6 5	
	6| 4		5	

	C	D7	Em	
1st voice	7| 4 4 6	5	5 5	5 ⸒ .||
	6|	5 4	4	
2nd voice	7| 3 3 5	4 3	3	⸒ .||
	6|	4	3 3	3

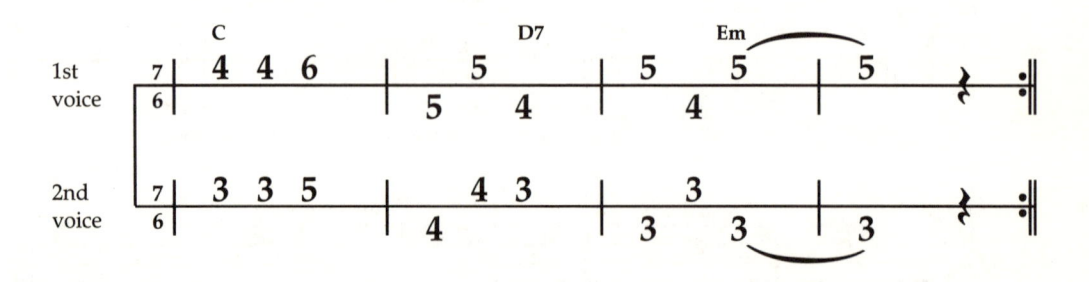